You GOal Girl!

JORGIE FRANKS
THE GOAL GIRL

Foreword by
Dr. Degrando Franks Jr.

The
Ultimate Guide
to **Achieve**
All Your **Goals**

You GOal Girl! The Ultimate Guide to Achieve All Your Goals

TMMI PUBLISHING

You GOal Girl! The Ultimate Guide to Achieve All Your Goals

Taylor Made Me Publishing Book
A subsidiary of Taylor Made Me Inc.
PO Box 3861
Brandon, FL 33509

ISBN # 0-9768726-0-9

Cover Design: Luis Ramirez
Page Design & Typography: Luis Ramirez
Photography: Mariland Gray
Editor: Olivia Harris

PRINTED IN THE UNITED STATES OF AMERICA
FIRST TAYLOR MADE ME PUBLISHING: April 2005

This book is available at quantity discounts for bulk purchases. For
additional information regarding TAYLOR MADE ME, INC.,
visit us on the web at **http://www.jorgiefranks.com**
or email us at **info@jorgiefranks**

You Goal Girl!
The Ultimate Guide to Achieve ALL Your Goals

Acknowledgements Page

To my Father. You wrote a powerful foreword, you have been tremendously supportive. You are not only my Father, but my Pastor. Thank you for working overtime raising a daughter like me. Thanks for your dedication, love, and wisdom.

To my Mother. Thanks for being my manager and my life line. I know I can always call on you for love and support. You have truly showed me what a virtuous woman is all about.

To my Brothers.
Dee, you are my big brother but still younger, remember that I love you, Preacher.
Philip, member of the young ones; do not forget me when you are a big time gospel rap artist.

To my mentor, Delatorro McNeal II. You are truly a blessing from above used to catapult my ministry. What can I say? For a small investment, you helped launch Taylor Made Me, Inc. and You GOal Girl! Thanks Del and Nova for the dedication you have shown to all of us. I met my speaking family right here with you. My brothers Anwar Richardson, Omicron Long, and Frederick Gray have stayed there encouraging me. Anwar, thanks for teaching me to live a life of excellence by your example. Omicron, you are an amazing educator and soldier. You have showed me how to be a strong soldier especially when obstacles come. Fred, you are a passionate person and your heart is right. I appreciate that. Donna Hicks Mitchell, thanks for being a mentor and guide for me. It is always good to have someone close to you who is so cool and together. I love knowing you and really appreciate you advice. Thanks.

To International Harvest Center Church of God, my church home. I appreciate you. Ever since I moved to Florida we have been through a lot together. You have encouraged me and truly been there for me through thick and thin. Your love is contagious. Also thanks to Church of God International for continuous support.

To Taylor's Godparents and some of my closest friends. Ashley Franks, Kristy Graciano, Ellyon Bell, and Mose and Davida Smith. You are truly special to me. Thanks for making this book possible.

To Katharis Gadson. Taylor is truly a blessing.

To Keona Williams. Thanks for being a true friend. You are my girl and I want to give a special acknowledgment to you and your beautiful family from Chief all the way down to lil' toot toot.

To several men and women who have served as extended moms and dads to me. Grandma Helen, Grandpa Degrando Sr., Uncle Herb, Uncle Duane, Uncle Keith, Uncle Robert, Aunt Marilyn, Aunt Betty, Aunt Sherry, Aunt Cynthia, Aunt Cebel, Uncle James, Aunt Denise, Uncle William, Lillian Lima (Oeration MOAR), Tametryce Collins, Sis. Lynette Brown, Stella Canty, Tyrone Keys (All Sports Community Service), Kim Norton, Mary Dillworth, Sis. Beverly Solomon and all my friends and family.

Foreward by Dr. Degrando Franks Jr.

Many times in the course of human struggle and frustrations we become extremely aware and learn to focus on the causes of our failure. We become accustomed to the making of excuses, the giving of reasons and settling for second best.

Our goal then becomes survival rather than success, trying rather than triumph, and endurance rather than accomplishment. It is the nature of man to settle rather than struggle, to compromise rather than compete and to cooperate rather than confront. The problem is that we have not learned how to become over-comers. How then do we change the course of failure and begin to win in life?

It has been aptly said, "If you give a man a fish, he'll eat for a day, but if you teach him to fish, he'll eat for a lifetime".

I believe that the way to change our direction in life is to change the knowledge we ingest and the application thereof.

Today, you have the opportunity to change your life forever.

Enclosed in the pages of this book is the author's step-by-step instruction on how to be extremely successful. I have found the secret to successfully changing many of today's ills is by setting appropriate goals, working those goals and coupling said goals with character, morality and integrity. I believe with out a shadow of a doubt that Jorgie Franks is one of today's most gifted young up and coming author's, speakers and a living example of how exciting life can be if you have the proper roadmap to success.

As her pastor and father, I completely endorse, "The GOal Girl."

Table of Contents

You GOal Girl: The Ultimate Guide to Achieve all your Goals

Dear Goal Achievers,

I want to thank you for taking the first step toward achieving your goals. I want you to understand me and maybe you will understand this timely message. I thank God for the opportunity to reach everyone all over the world and impact lives. I thank God for preparing me to be a vessel and using me. I thank God for equipping me to help people attain their goals with passion and drive. God is number one in my life and the source of my strength. He is my all in all and He is all I have ever known.

I was raised in the church and I am sure some of you were also. My father, Dr. Degrando Franks Jr. is a pastor which makes me a preacher's kid PK. A lot of famous stars began their talents in the church, such as, Jessica Simpson, George Bush, Denzel Washington, Beyonce, and Dr. Martin Luther King Jr. We all know these abovementioned and even more out there are thanking God for their accomplishments. I tried to bridle my passion for Christ so that this book and my message would be more accepted in the mainstream. I started to preach a couple times in this book, then I realized I don't need to be accepted, I need to tell the truth and be committed to changing the lives of others.

Overall, I have your best interest at heart and I want you to achieve your goals and whatever God called you to do. With God all things are possible. If you are truly serious about your goals, dream, purpose, passions, and visions you will continue to read and enjoy this life changing experience.

John 15:16, 17 Amplified Bible (AMP)

You have not chosen Me, but I have chosen YOU and appointed YOU [I have planted you], that you might GO and bear fruit and keep bearing, and that your fruit may be lasting [that it may abide], so whatever you ask the Father in My Name [as presenting all that I AM], He may give it to you. This is what I command you that you love one another.

Galatians 5:22, 23 New International Version (NIV)

But the fruit of the Spirit is love, joy, peace, patience, kindness, goodness, faithfulness, gentleness, and self-control. Against such things there is no law.

Achieving my goals and helping you achieve yours,
Jorgie Franks "The Goal Girl"

You Goal Girl
The Ultimate Guide to Achieve all your Goals

By Jorgie Franks
"The Goal Girl"

Dedication Page

I dedicate this book to God for making it possible and showing me your will is so much better.

I dedicate this book to Taylor, my daughter. I dedicate this book to you because you gave me the motivation to go after my goals. I love you, cutie pie.

Section 1: 15 Excuses

Excuses are something we all have in common. As I was about to begin Bible Study at my church I was prepared to teach my class about excuses and admonish them not to make excuses. One girl in my class raises her hand and says, "I just got suspended off the bus." I say, "Why?" She yells, "It's not my fault." A characteristic of an excuse is defending her and blaming others. I went on to ask her what happened and she said a boy threw a ball of paper at her and she threw it back at him. This is the real reason she got suspended. Blaming someone was an excuse she used. Since she didn't use the truthful reason because she doesn't like the truth, or didn't think the truth was good enough; she made an excuse.

Is an excuse a lie? Well in that same class a young lady kept looking down at her lap. I thought she was dozing off so I kept beckoning for her attention. My assistant says to her, "Are you tired?" She says, "Yes I am so sleepy," and then she drops her cell phone. Truth be told, she was text messaging her boyfriend. I would say her excuse for looking down was a lie. When polling youth and adults, excuses are negative. An excuse is usually not thought of as a reason but instead thought of as a lie. Usually a person is going to give a truthful reason and if they don't have one, they will make up an excuse. In most cases we use excuses to justify why we are not doing something that we are very capable of doing.

"YOU GOal Girl!" was created to encourage you to go after your goals no matter what you are going through. One way to not accomplish your goals is to make excuses. There is no excuse for living a mediocre life. You are called to be above and not beneath. It will truly change your life if you make a conscious effort to stop making excuses. As you read this book you will be able to identify the following: some of the most common excuses, the reasons we make them, and how to stop making them. Remember there are no excuses for not reaching your goals, dreams, passions, and purpose.

"I don't have time."

Who does? We all have planners and try to stick to a schedule. Just because we fail to stick to our planners and schedules doesn't allow us to use this common excuse. Why? You have the time; however, you are not using your time correctly. It is not easy but it is not an excuse. You have the time. Sometimes the time is right in front of you but instead you decide to do other things. I find myself sitting in front of the TV and complaining about not having time to fold my laundry. Sometimes the remedy for "I don't have time" is to multi-task.

2."I am a single parent."
You still can achieve your destiny. I am twenty-three, a single mother, and I have used my child as an excuse. First, I have to spend a lot of money on my child. Childcare, diapers, baby wipes, baby food, burp cloths, they all add up. Then as my baby grows there are even more expenses. Oftentimes we are forced to raise our children with little or no support. For instance, your goal may to be a doctor or become a business owner. A child comes and it seems like there isn't any time to accomplish this goal. It seems like there aren't any funds either.

You may ask, "How do I go to school, study, and finance my dreams." There is a way. Somehow you can do it. It is up to you to figure it out. Alternative ideas to achieve your goals as a single parent:

"PK" Moment: Remember God can and will provide all your needs according to his riches in glory.

- Ask for help- I am always calling on Taylor's four Godmothers and Godfathers to give me some help. They are such a blessing.

- Establish a savings-Even if it is just in your top drawer. There are financial advisors and also computer programs that can help you track your savings.
- Clip Coupons-One time I went to the grocery store and they forgot to ring up my receipts. Imagine my joy when at the end of the transaction they just rang up the coupons and gave me cash. It was then when I realized the coupons were as good as cash.
- Research social service programs
- Research financial assistance for college
- Get support from your partner even if it requires going the legal route!

3. I cannot afford it.
We often find creative ways to get things we really want. For example, my goal was to become a professional speaker. My first business cards cost $12. Now my business cards require a photo shoot. So basically ask yourself: "What can I afford now and how can I afford more later?" Start there and that is how you gradually achieve more success.

4.One day!
Grandma said it best when she said,
•"Today is the day."

- "Tomorrow might be too late."
- "Seize the day."
- "Why put off until tomorrow what you can do today."
- "Time is of the essence"

And most importantly "There is no better time than the present."

5. It is too late in life.

It is never too late. When we feel this way it means you have to work harder, faster and sooner! It means we cannot make excuses anymore but instead we have to do it now. Go right now and make a game plan. Set your goals in order to meet your dreams. Then tell a young person your testimonial and tell them, "YOU GO!" Encouraging others oftentimes builds the confidence and motivation we need in ourselves.

Who can encourage you today?

_____

_____

6. "I don't know how."

Soon as I began to share my dream with others and tell them what I wanted to do in life I realized that most people out there have dreams and goals of their own. I am sure you are one of those people. You have a book that you want to write, a dance class you want to take, or a city you want to visit. For every idea and dream you have there is a way to achieve it. You can do it and oftentimes, others will give you help as well. They will assist you; some for free and some for a price. It is not anyone else's job to share with you what they learned so if they do, take notes and pay attention. Do not take anyone or any one's help for granted. Others can and will help but ultimately it is your responsibility to figure out how to achieve your goals.

7. "I don't feel good."

There is a difference between being sick one day and being sick as an excuse. Do whatever you can to overcome your sickness. Imagine if the world was ran by people who don't feel like it or don't feel good. Really think about it. A bunch of sadness, complaining, and we probably wouldn't be getting too far. I don't feel good is not a good excuse at all. Think about all the people who have diseases but work everyday for their insurance. There is always someone out there who has it worse than you. I am not trying to disregard your feelings. Please think about some ways you can cope.

What are some ways to lift your spirit?

_____

_____

Some ways you can cope is turn on some good music. List the things
you have going for you. Also if you feel down there are options to bring
your spirits higher. I believe my faith in God helps me tremendously.
I have hope and believe I can accomplish anything. Also, yoga and
exercise boost confidence and energy. I love writing in my online journal
and sometimes I will e-mail my entry to someone who cares for me.
Sometimes talking to someone who has already gone through some of
your trials can help, but overall you must take responsibility. You are the
one who will have to call a support group or doctor. You will have to
read uplifting books and get up for church. Don't use this as an excuse
to be defeated. You can overcome that feeling one step at a time. The
importance is making a step.
What are some preventative things you can do to avoid bad feelings?

_____

_____

8. "I work too much."
Try being a mother of 13 and working full-time. Sojourner Truth did that
and still was a big activist. Try being a father confined to a wheel chair.
Try being a full-time student in six extra-curricular activities trying to
maintain an honor's status. I could go on and on with stories of people
who are achieving significant things in their life and the lives of others.
Let's focus on your significant, world changing story. Remember you
want to have one. Remember you are working for a reason. I know
you may not want to hear this BUT sometimes accomplishing a goal
is like working too much and working another job. Remember though,
YOU make your goals and no one else, so don't let the extra work you
do discourage you. It is something that you wanted and you are in the
process of making it happen.
9. "I'm tired."
Oh you better get used to it! I am not an advocator of caffeine. Anything
addictive cannot be good unless it is addiction to achieving your goal.
I encourage trying to get more sleep at night. Also, go walking or do
jumping jacks. Find what works for you. The point "I'm tired" never

works. It never got anyone that sought after a job, a college degree, or a house with a backyard. Everyone is tired at a point but it cannot stop you. Set a goal that says, for instance, I will not go to sleep until I finish all the laundry. Your clearly stated ambitions will eliminate all excuses! "You GOal Girl!" is a saying to energize and encourage you. It means I am proud of you and keep up the good work. This drive to progress will eliminate, "I'm tired." What works for me is praying when I feel weak.

"PK" Moment: Nehemiah 8:10 The joy of the Lord is your strength.

10. I can't do it.

People say this before they even try. In college when I was working full-time, and going to school full-time there was times where I used this excuse. I am not proud of this but I did. Life felt so overwhelming and I could not see how I was going to get through it. Just because you cannot see it, doesn't mean it can't happen. When you feel like you cannot do it don't talk about it, be about it. Instead of focusing on what you are going through, focus on where and what you are going to. Put forth all the effort you have because you only have one life. What are you holding back for? You can do it and when you feel like you can't, don't talk about it.

"PK" Moment: Talk to God if you need to talk. Focus that energy on what you can do.

5

11. "Good things don't happen to me."

Good things can and will happen to you. You must change your mindset. You must expect good things to come your way. You are consistently working to achieve your goals, and you will achieve them. No one else will have confidence in you if you don't have confidence in yourself. What is something good that happened to you recently?

_____

_____

12. "I just want to be average"

I am a preacher's kid and I grew up in the church. I was always taught that I am more than a conqueror. Mediocrity or this C mentality is "stinkin' thinkin'". I don't need an A or B, just a C. Whatever! Please list what is good about being average. In school, students use this comment as an excuse to just get by and not excel in anything. I want to be average is an excuse not to find your niche or purpose but instead master in nothing and be OK (average) in everything. I am here to tell you, you are above average. You are extraordinary. It is your time. Your time is now to excel in anything you put your mind to. Be persistent and full of life. You GO!

13. "I am afraid to fail."

The biggest failure is quitting. Don't do it. Just think about school, to fail you must have just totally missed class or not even try. Failure is negative so at least try. If this is your dream and passion, try or you will miss out. If God has given you the vision, he will give you the provision and provide for you. You

"PK" Moment: Psalms 37:4 God will give you the desires of your heart. Hebrews 11:1 Now faith is the substance of things hoped for and the evidence of things not seen. The Bible says you have to have faith the size of a mustard seed.

have to believe that whatever is in your heart to accomplish will and can happen. Have faith in yourself; you can do it. All you need is a little faith and God will open the door for so much more.

14. "My parents never showed me how."

Everyone likes to play in the blame game, even I do occasionally. Perhaps the biggest blame targets are parents. Since I am a mother I really understand that parents don't have a manual they just do the best they know how. It could be that your parents didn't teach you something because they were never taught how. This is why it is important not to use your parents as your excuse but instead learn whatever lessons you can from your parents and then either apply them or simply take a side note that what they may have done you definitely do not want to do.

This applies to others in our lives as well especially those who raised you or had a major influence in your development. This could be grandparents, aunts, uncles, and siblings, and even friends. So just in case you didn't get it, these people are not an excuse. If they were not the best in your eyes you may just have to work just a little harder, at

"PK" Moment: God has a lot to say about parenting, it is wise to know what he says.

least you have an example of what not to do. And if they did well, take notes and learn. The Bible says in Exodus 20:12, the first commandment with promise is honoring your parents. It even goes far enough to say if you curse your parents you will die (check Matthew 15:4.) Parents

are supporters, protectors, leaders, and guides. God's direction flows through parents, especially godly parents. God holds parents in a high esteem and so should you. In your decisions also remember one day you may be that parent wanting to be held up in high esteem.

15. It is too hard.

"I have all these things stacked up against me." "No one is helping me." Sometimes it is hard but you do have to learn how to turn lemons to lemonade. Try not to complain and continue to work hard. Anything worth having is worth working for. I am pleased with the outcome of the things I have worked really hard for. I have my degree, my youth pastor position, my book, my dream, and my beautiful daughter. Sometimes things do get hard and feelings of doubt creep in. However, I am always comforted in the knowledge that if I just keep on pressing forward, it will get easier

"PK" Moment: I have heard the song several times that says, "I won't complain because when I look around and I think things over my good days outweigh my bad days, I won't complain. God's been so good to me."

8 Types of Goals

1. Finances

Sometimes when it comes to finances we don't really know where to go next. That is why I believe in making financial goals. I believe you should educate yourself on finances and then from there make goals that will help you in other areas. For instance, my goal is to buy a house. So I make other financial goals like pay off credit card debt, save an emergency fund, go to first time homebuyers classes to get a grant, maintain budget (I get to check this one off if I maintain it for 3 months), and get a daytime career. The financial goal may be to cut back on wasteful spending. You may set a financial goal like, "No more purses or expensive jewelry." Some may even make a financial goal to pay tithes and offering to their local church, make a financial contribution to a charity, or community organization. These goals in finances can be the maker or breaker, because almost every big dream in our hearts cost money. So to discipline yourself in this area, set and maintain goals. Regarding finances, what are your strengths?

_____

_____

What are your weaknesses?

_____

_____

2. Personal Development

YOU are important. Make sure YOU are cultivating yourself in goal setting. YOU want to become all that YOU can be by setting goals to improve who and what YOU are. I believe that sometimes we concern ourselves so much with other people that we forget how we are developing. Are we reaching our destiny? Are we stronger today than yesterday? We don't examine our decisions and ourselves and therefore our personal development lacks. Everyday we should be making large strides to develop ourselves.

What have you done today to change your tomorrow?

_____

_____

3. Relationships

Relationships always need to be under evaluation. We, as goal achievers, need to be careful whom we yoke up to. Yoke means join up with or connect with. When something is yoked it is pretty secure. We need to make sure if we are jumping in a relationship it is the right person to yoke up with.

You can ask yourself the following questions:
1. Is this person selfish?
2. Am I going to uplift this person?
3. Are they going to uplift me?

In any relationship be very careful because everyone is not looking out for you. What usually happens is they are looking out for their interest only. For instance, I was with my daughter's father for 2 years. He was a very selfish person. He wanted me to be there for him through good and bad but when it came time for him to be there for my daughter and I, he was gone physically. During this time loved ones who I had long standing relationships with told me he was not the man God has ordained for me however, I chose to help God out. In relationships especially with the opposite sex you have to determine if that person really deserves you. On top of that you must evaluate and listen to those who you have stronger and longer relationships with you because they will look at your situation a bit more objective. The subjectivity comes in because they are looking out for you.

Who are you yoked to?

> *"PK" Moment: Establish a relationship with God first then establish a relationship with man, especially when you are single.*

> *"PK" Moment: The Bible says you need to guard your heart because out of it flows the issues of life.*

_____

_____

If you are a single parent, what relationship do you want with your child's other parent and how sure are you?

_____

_____

_____

_____

4. Extracurricular Activities, Volunteer Work, or Professional Organizations
It is very good to get involved. Most organizations are built to make you stronger and develop your goals. Professional organizations are great because they help you sharpen your skills. Volunteering is great; you can make a difference in someone else's life. I love mentoring the youth at my church. I take time to help with reading skills and personal development. You can make a huge difference by visiting an elderly person at their home for help. Just get involved. You are giving of your time and please believe you reap what you sow. Good deeds will come back to you. Extra-curricular is just that; extra ways to grow and learn. These three facets are there as extra ways to help you reach your goals. Why do you volunteer?

_____

_____

Are you in any organizations that help you achieve your goals at a higher level?

_____

_____

5. House cleaning
I had to add this because whether you are ten and live with your parents, twenty and live in an apartment, dorm or thirty and own a home. Housecleaning is vital. This sometimes dreaded area is part of self-improvement. In this area a goal that you can set is making your bed daily (maintained it for 3 months straight, I can cross it out). Clean the carpet and vacuum the stairs are good ones. Whatever the need in your home, make it a goal and maintain it. It is up to you! There is no need to

settle in this area. Constantly making improvements will stop problems from occuring.

What does your living space say about you?

_____

_____

Is that what you want it to say?

_____

_____

6. Physical Health
This is vital. How long do you want to live? This question is so important because how are you going to live a long life if you are not taking care of your body. Your body represents the essence of who you are. Unfortunately people cannot know your heart before they see you. How do you want people to see you when they look at you? Online there are so many tips on how to improve your physical health. Start with using a search engine like Google or Dogpile and type in wellness, or physical health.

"PK" Moment: You must have control over your flesh and not let it rule you.

7. Spirituality
These types of goals are an inspiration to me personally. I try to excel in my spiritual life by reading books and surrounding myself with positive people. I have an ongoing goal of being in church on Sunday's and Wednesday's. I accepted God into my heart and I try to live a life that is pleasing to him. Some people who are not as spiritual as me make a goal to go to church every Sunday. Some people want to be an usher or just watch church on television. Whatever your goals are spiritually it is best if you can stick with it and not be distracted.

"PK" Moment: If you are faithful in a few things God will make you ruler over many.

Who or what do you put before God?

_____

_____

8. "Taylor Time"

This is a time I spend with just my daughter, Taylor. I try to set goals in this area so that even when I am tired or busy, I always have "Taylor Time." Even if it is just for a hour or two or to give her a bath and do her hair. During "Taylor Time," no one else but Taylor and I are included. If you are a parent this time benefits you because it helps you focus on your goals and gives you a good sense of who you are and what your motivations are. "Taylor Time" also represents the quality time you make for those closest to you. It is time you set aside for those who need you whether it is friends, family, or others. For me "Taylor Time" is for Taylor.

Who is your "Taylor Time" for?

_____

_____

Who needs more of you in their life?

_____

_____

Who needs less of you in their life?

_____

_____

5 $\mathcal{W}$ays to Diversify

1. It is good to just list all your dreams and goals. Set your long-term dreams and short-term dreams leaving nothing out. Some say list 30 things you would do if you could not fail. I say list as many things as you can if you couldn't fail. It is up you to make your goals and dreams become a reality.

2. I have a list hanging in my room of goals I want completed. The top three goals need to be completed by the end of the year and the rest need to be completed as soon as possible. I look at them all the time. I cannot avoid them. They are on my wall. My goals are more important than any basketball player or celebrity. I do not want to avoid my goals because they are my dreams. They are my nuggets for success. I am very excited every time I get to cross a completed goal off my list.

3. Be creative. I know I am. I have a house book. This book includes paste pictures of the goals I want to achieve. I call it the house book because it outlines achieving my goal to be a homeowner. If you are about to get married or are considering marriage, you can make a wedding book. If you are working on your finances you could make a money book including articles, photos, and tips on finances. There are so many different things you can do to achieve your goals.

4. Use simple, borderline "to-do list" goals (i.e. clean room) and also mission statement goals. For example, write a book geared towards motivating the world to go for their goals. That way one of your goals is constantly being checked off the list and you are being challenged. You Go!

5. I make sure to write an ideal date but never beat yourself up if you do not make that date. You must never beat yourself up if you do not meet a goal date on time because you cannot give up. You must constantly keep going for your goals. One of the best things about dates is pressure. I am one of those people who work really well under pressure. I had to condition myself in college to manage my time so that I didn't always wait until the last minute to finish things. I always procrastinated because that way I knew it would get done. I know now procrastination is unacceptable. Practice accomplishing your goals in the time designated. Eventually it will be a cinch.

Worksheet to Diversify your Goals
(This will help you with creative goals.)
What exotic country do you want to travel to?

_____

_____

What outfit have you always wanted to wear?

_____

_____

Have you ever wanted to go to a day spa? *(Pamper yourself.)*

_____

_____

Have your always wondered what happened to a particular friend from high school?

_____

_____

Do you have artistic ability to help cultivate your goals? (i.e. rap your goals, poem of goals, scrapbook of goals) How can you capture your goals in a fun way?

_____

_____

Do you have short term and long term goals?

_____

_____

Do you work well under pressure?

_____

_____

What are simple goals you know you can accomplish now to help meet a bigger goal?

_____

_____

10 $\mathcal{T}$en Destructive Don'ts

Keep in mind that "Don'ts" are not the fun part of life. "Don't chew with your mouth open." "Don't talk when the teacher is talking." "Don't come to work late." The word don't is a disciplinary word. Not too many people can say discipline is their favorite. We usually hear do not do something because the short cut is a lot easier. Has anyone ever gave you direction and said, "Whatever you do, do not make the first right." "Whatever you do, do not travel in that area at night." It is hazardous not to follow these don'ts. In making and achieving goals in life it is just as hazardous not to follow the don'ts. Listen to these don'ts and avoid hazard by listening to the warnings.

"PK" Moment: Proverbs 18:21 (NIV) The tongue has the power of life and death...

1. Don't make excuses (Please see section 1) This DON'T is so big; it had to have its own section. This had to be addressed quickly in the book because there is no excuse that you are not living your dreams. You dictate to your life what will happen. Just like you can dictate to someone what to do, you can dictate to your life what is going to happen to you. You have to be strong and of good courage. You must believe in yourself and grasp the strength of your word. There is no excuse for not going all the way and pulling all the stops for your goals. If you work on a job you can agree by being employed to show up in the snow and sometimes in a hurricane. You have to show up when you are sick and when you're loved ones are sick. So if there is something you want for you and your family, Why aren't you willing to do 10 times more to get it? Why bother making an excuse if it is for your dream. Save the excuses for your employer (Joke).

"PK" Moment: There are numerous times in the Bible where God emphasized how pleased he was when we loved him and followed him wholeheartedly. Ephesians 6:7 (NIV) Serve wholeheartedly as if you are serving God, not man. In all things do it as unto the Lord

What excuses do you use?

_____

_____

2. Don't give up

If it is really easy for you to give up, it was never a real goal to begin with. If it is a desire it is a goal. If you have a real passion for achievement, it is a goal. If someone can just talk you out of your passion there is a problem. Most likely you are dealing with a mere idea, not the real thing. When it is goal time you do and learn whatever you need to, to achieve it. There are several times when I went to make a goal and for certain reasons I did not attain them. For instance, I made five goals to have achieved by the year 2003.

1. To be a motivational speaker, corporate trainer, or spokesperson for a   fortune 500 company.
2. To own a house.
3. To be student government president.
4. To read the whole Bible
5. To write a book.

I am a professional speaker. I am saving for a new house to be bought in 2005. I didn't make it as student government president. I continue to make goals. I will never stop until I die. You were put on this earth for a particular purpose. Don't give up on it. If you haven't discovered it yet, don't give up because it is right around the corner. Be encouraged. Encourage yourself. Don't give up. That is how this book was inspired. Keep on going for your goals. You Go! God is with you. Even when you feel like there is no hope, don't give up. You may have to make some minor alterations on a goal. Don't take it too personal. Don't give up.

I am not perfect. Writing this book does not guarantee that I will accomplish all of my goals. I do however give the guarantee I will not give up. You will get new ideas and tips. Get a notebook and write some new goals but don't give up. Some major players in the professional

"PK" Moment: There is no doubt that the #1 inspirational book is The Holy Bible.

speaking industry will tell you when making goals don't write goals you have already accomplished but sometimes it is good to re-list the goals you have accomplished so you are motivated to accomplish the new goals. For example, I completed College with a 3.1 G.P.A and 3.6 in my major. This was important to me. I received a grant for down payment on my first home. The goals that I have accomplished can go on the wall next to your other goals to encourage you not to give up.

3. Don't talk about it, be about it.
"Bonus! Bonus! Bonus!"
Don't procrastinate, Initiate and overall prove It!
This is so important. These "don'ts" actually determine your life. You have to seize the moment. Don't put off your dreams and goals. Take the steps now that you need to take. It is vital not to just say things you do not mean. If you talk, shouldn't it be meaningful? So what is the point in saying it if you are not willing to take the steps to make it come to pass? How many times have you said, I need to do my laundry, and then watch a movie, lie down, or go shopping. This is inexcusable behavior and a truly bad habit. If you think it, write it down. If you talk about it or say you need to do it, be about it. When I say be about it…Abide in it, Act on it, Breathe it, Continue to work on it, Endure through it, Prevail it, Obtain it, Remain, Stand, Stay, Survive, Conquer, Love, Excel, Outplay, Outshine, Outrun, Overtake, Triumph, Surpass, BECOME, grow into, mature, shift, turn into, display, and make it happen.

I tell people my goals all the time. People I love and some people I don't even know, can dictate my dreams. Almost every time without fail, within 5 seconds they say I need to write a book, or I want to be a motivational speaker. They have all these wonderful ideas but do not put them to use. It is not easy but just sitting back is not going to get a book written. Just talking about Missy Elliot's diamonds are not going to get you any. So here we go again, when making goals we cannot just talk about it, but we have to do it, be about it. We cannot say, "I will start tomorrow." We have to do it today, now! This is a serious matter. This is not a joke. These are your goals.

Bonus! Bonus! Bonus! Don't Procrastinate, Initiate. This means don't procrastinate at all. Don't put off, Do it now and Don't stop. Initiate a plan and initiate yourself. You Go!

4. Don't blame others.
If your goals are laying on the wayside, it is your fault. Time to take responsibility. As we go through things in life we have to hold on to our goals and dreams. It is no ones responsibility but yours to make it happen. I have tried to blame others so many times. Just yesterday I was blaming my daughter because she wouldn't go to sleep so I couldn't do

anything. I am living with my parents so I did not have enough space to do what I needed to do. I was blaming people and the predicament I was in. Realizing that these predicaments are predicaments I put myself in. I cannot blame anyone for anything. The Lord is in control of all, but you have to take responsibility for the decisions you make and the way you use your time. Maybe instead of blaming my daughter, I should get a babysitter and go to library,. The only way this book will get finished and my goals accomplished is if I stop blaming others for my living conditions, my cleanliness, my daughter, my schedule, and my responsibilities. I am sorry but blaming others is not an option. It is on me and it is on you.

Who cares more about you than you? Not others so why are we blaming them. Some say don't tell people your goals but I say tell everyone. People will remind you if they are not done. Enemies may talk trash and discourage you if you don't complete them. Some of your best cheerleaders are your enemies. Don't blame your enemies if you don't live out your dreams or live up to your expectations. You have to make the comeback for the decisions you made, not them. Please use wisdom, you do not want to share detailed goals with your sometimes shady associates but I don't see anything wrong with sharing your general goals. For instance, tell them your goal is to have your book published by September. Don't tell them the name and content, just the basics. Are you following me? My daughters' childcare provider Dorothy Drew taught me a powerful lesson regarding people. Unfortunately there are truly people who

18

"PK" Moment: "The enemy doesn't miss a trick," she says. "Beware, Be honest, but Be wise in Christ."

are considered dream killers. They are out there and they are poisonous. They will say, "I thought you were writing a book, Where is it?" I am excited about your dream and I want to see you succeed. The better you do the more adversity will come. However, stay focused and don't blame others. Everyone will not understand or see your vision but they will when you achieve your goals. Now, YOU GO!

Who are you blaming?

_____

_____

5. Don't talk about a goal you are not serious about.
I want you to get used to using power. One of the biggest power tools you have is your tongue and the words that come out of your mouth. If you are just saying that you want something and you are not willing to work for it really, leave it alone and don't talk about it. But if you really want it and believe it by all means, tell the world. If it is really easy for you to give up, it was never a goal to begin with. Your ideas are important. There is a huge difference between an idea and a goal. An idea is a wonderful and sometimes powerful suggestion but a goal is acted upon. A goal is the POW in Power. Without the POW you are sitting around saying, "er uh," POW represents action. When you think of POW, dynamite comes to mind and we do not need to blow up things, but we do need to have power. With a goal you have the plan.
Are you living powerful?

_____

_____

We all have talked about goals that are not serious, have you? What are your play goals?

_____

_____

6. Don't let your personal appearance limit your personal achievement (Don't say you are too big, small, or too tall or short.)
I remember for a long period in my life I felt as though I was too tall. Yes, me. I didn't like to stand near guys who were short and I especially didn't want to go out with a man who was my height or shorter. One day I realized that I have to work my height out for my advantage. I realized that this insecurity of mine could be limiting me. For instance, I didn't want to wear heels because I might be taller than the guy. I realized my goal to look professional and successful was not being fulfilled so I bought heels that were shorter to wear and on special occasions I will pull out my pumps. I allowed my height to hold me back from accomplishing some goals. Keep in mind we all come in different shapes and sizes and you may be able to set small goals to slowly cut the pounds off. Small goals such as running 15 minutes, 4 days a week or big goals like running for an hour and then do the Stairmaster for an hour. Don't let your personal appearance limit your personal achievement.

Is there anything about your life or personal appearance that you feel limits you?

_____

_____

What are some of your goals you need to make to improve in this area?

_____

_____

7. Don't let your day job interfere with your goals.

I have had big dreams since I was a child. I was one of those people who knew I had big dreams. I have worked since I was 15, so I assumed that I was always going to have to work for someone else. This is such a false, yet sad way of believing. I had far more to give than that. All the dreams and goals could be accomplished while I was working. I have to work 90 hours a week versus 40 but it is worth it to achieve my goals. The biggest mistake people make is they quit their full time job before they are making at least that in their goal or dream job. You have to hustle! Go! Go! Go! If it is important to you, you can't stop. Work at your day job full-time and your dream part-time. Do your best at both.

What are your goals for your day job?

_____

_____

If you had to open your own company what would it consist of?

_____

_____

8. Don't compare yourself to others.

Just like there is no two fingerprints there is not another YOU anywhere. So it is not good to compare yourself to something or someone completely different. God made you a beautiful unique individual with your own flair. Now it is up to you to figure out your flairs and walk confidently in them. A goal you can set in this area is making a list of all the things you enjoy, and are good at. Make sure to acknowledge that no two people do something exactly alike so do the best that you can. What you can do is, do (Your name goes here) the best you can.

What is great about you? *(you need extra lines for this one)*

_____

_____

_____

_____

_____

Who do you envy and why?

_____

_____

9. Don't be a "hater."

I try not to jump on the bandwagon of the latest fads and lingo but I have adopted this one. Don't be a hater but be a congratulator. Don't hate, participate. These phrases are just an encouragement not to be jealous and envious. When others are doing better than you, this is the game plan. If someone close to you or far away is doing better than you, some jealous tendencies may pop up. This is normal but you must control it. Just go to a local convenience store and buy a congratulations card and mail it or jump on the Internet and send a quick e-mail.

"PK" Moment: You need to ask for forgiveness, God said. Check Colossians 3:13.

Sometimes you can combat that negative energy with positive and shame the devil.

Second Game Plan is to participate. For instance, your best friend finishes his or her college degree before you when you started at the same time. You feel a little animosity because you feel behind and instead of congratulating; you withdraw from him or her. You chose not to bust your butt and you allowed yourself to become distracted from your goals. Now your friendship is struggling because of your mistakes. In this predicament, your best bet is to participate in overtime. Work ten times harder to finish school and to call your friend in spite of your feelings. Go to the graduation. If this is a real close friend you might even tell him or her how you feel. Please cut down on your dosage of "haterade."

Who have you hated on lately? How can you make it right?

_____

_____

Who are the "haters" in your life right now?

_____

_____

Who do you need to beware of?

_____

_____

10. Don't get distracted.

When I say don't get distracted I am so serious. This is one of the major
don'ts. The reason for this is we have so many people out there who
have great ideas with powerful potential but everytime you are about
to break loose the chains and go to the next level, a distraction comes.
For me, I was in college, I just graduated with my Associates degree in
Mass Communications and I got involved with this man and he totally
rearranged my life. My Goals to be involved in school and do these
great feats at church were postponed because this beautiful man who
seemed to have all the answers distracted me. Imagine my surprise when
I ended up pregnant and he was gone when our daughter was 2 months
old. I thank God for my beautiful daughter but surely I could have done
without the distraction. I have found one of my major distractions to be
men. For you, it could be women, your parents, or even something like
music, TV, or shopping. If I told you this one distraction could keep you
from your destiny. Would you let it go?
What are your distractions?

_____

_____

15 *𝒟ynamic Do's*

Now that the don'ts are out the way, the do's are a little easier on you. This list gives you what to accomplish and guideline to use to perform your goals. When I speak in schools the student always want don'ts first and do's second. Save the best for last.

1. Do put your goals everywhere.

This is so big. The more you see and acknowledge your goals the more times it is ingrained in you and becomes more apart of you. Do put your goals in places you see often and discover a new creative way everyday. This fun activity will keep your creative juices flowing. (Please see Section 6.)

2. Do invest in yourself.

Your biggest investment in life is in you. When you are strong, you can really help others. I am encouraging you to invest in your self financially, spiritually, physically, emotionally, and in any way that will improve your integrity and character. I learned this financial principle from my mom. It seems every time I get a new job it costs money. When I got a job at a jewelry store I needed a suit so she bought me 3. When I got a job working in a check-cashing store I needed black pants and she bought me 3 pair. She was investing in my future and it taught me in big and small ways I should to. This Do is so important because the return of investing in you is very high. Only because you know you and you know your hopes and dreams. Only YOU hold the power to cultivate them.

3. Do cut off the TV

This "Do" is a gold mine. Television is so exciting. You can buy cable and receive over one hundred channels. On some networks or satellite you can get over six hundred channels. I am not saying do not get these channels but I am admonishing you to turn the television off. Do make time for other things. Do not let the television distract you from completing your goals. It is so easy to sit in front of a good television show and let your thoughts and dreams escape you. Next time your goal is to exercise, do cut off the TV. If your goal is to write a book or article, do cut off the TV. If your goal is to spend quality time with a loved one, do cut off the TV. If your goal is to clean, do turn off the TV. You can even make a deal with yourself. Let's say your favorite show comes on at 8:30 so you have to complete your task prior to that time. Sometimes that one step will take you so much closer to achieving your goals. What are your favorite TV Shows?

_____

_____

What time do your favorite shows come on?

_____

_____

What is your favorite TV Network?

_____

_____

4. Do ask for help.
So many people are scared to ask for help. This one has always been hard for me to understand because I will ask for help in a heartbeat. You will really be surprised how many people have a heart to help. I have been in a predicament where I needed a babysitter for a situation and I had to ask for help. I did not want to at first because I felt like I was imposing but after I approached someone I trusted they were excited. Then I realized there was a whole pool of people who felt insulted because I would not ask for help. This same principle happens in all walks of life. For instance, at work when I needed to complete an assignment and I got lost or confused just asking for help made someone else feel useful or in demand and I was still able to complete my work.

The reason one of your goals may not be checked off is because you will not ask for help. For instance, in the case of setting a goal to lose a certain amount of weight, try asking for help. You have tried every diet on this side of the track but have you ever asked for help from a personal trainer, Weight Watchers, or Jenny Craig? Sometimes when you are trying to accomplish a goal, simply ask for help.

Who is on your support team? Why?

_____

_____

5. Do Rest

This is so you can have energy and stamina to reach the next level of success. Have you ever been around someone who is always yawning? I bet you do not perceive that person has it all together. I bet you are even confused if that person really even wants to hear what you are saying in a conversation. However, that person is tired. When you do not get enough rest it shows. People can look at you and think something is wrong with you just because you are tired. Some may even think you are older than you really are. I am sitting at work right now at 2:51 AM. I work the night shift and it is aging me. When I finally get home I will sleep about 4 or 5 hours which is what my body usually gets, and unfortunately it shows. Simple rest can help you feel more refreshed, relaxed, less tense, and more energized to achieve your goals.

How many hours of sleep do you get?

_____

_____

6. Do dress for success

Sometimes your attire can set you up to achieve your goals. I believe that sometimes the way we dress communicates before we even open our mouth. Ask yourself the question, "What does my attire communicate?" I hope that you will say that your attire is communicating confidence and class, professionalism and good taste. Sometimes when setting goals if you begin to dress the part, you will be in the mind frame to accomplish the goal. For instance, if you want to move up the corporate ladder, maybe your attire should move up to business from business casual. Maybe if you want to be a basketball player, buy basketball sneakers. Your dress can contribute to your success.

What outfits do you own that give you confidence and speak success?

_____

_____

What is successful dress in your business or the business you desire to work in?

_____

_____

7. Do network
The importance of networking is getting to know new people that can help and cultivate you while you help and cultivate them. It is an art to networking. It is more than just taking people's business cards but you have to keep in touch and inform them of your progress and check on theirs. You have to be action oriented; always making phone calls or writing e-mails. It is constant work but it is fun. If you are trying to reach a goal, try to network with people who have already achieved your goals. I believe there is a business network as well as a family network. I keep an address book compiled of family and friends. It is a good feeling to have family and friends call because they know you have everyone's number. Network also pays when I was raising money to go to a life changing professional speaking seminar. I sent out sponsorship letters and I received a great response because I was networking hard. The rewards of networking are more than business but also very personal.
How do you keep up with your business cards and contacts? How can you improve?

_____

_____

8. Do make quiet time for yourself
Sometimes in order to make a powerful profound impact on others and to achieve your goals you have to meditate and find quiet time for yourself. In this quiet time you may read or pray. You may draw or do something that is enjoyable to you but this time is for yourself. You may like to walk in the park or get on a swing but in this time you are not to be distracted. With me having quiet in my car gives me time to reflect.
Where do you go for quiet time?

_____

_____

9. Do believe in yourself

If YOU do not believe in yourself, who will?. Since this book is about YOU and YOUR goals I would say believing that YOU can achieve YOUR goals is vital. Notice I did not write, "Do think YOU can do it?" I specifically wrote believe because that puts all the pressure on YOU. If YOU know that even though it is not done yet, I can and

"PK" Moment: I want to live a life, pleasing in God's eyesight. I am longing to hear Matthew 25:23 His master replied, 'Well done, good and faithful servant! You have been faithful with a few things; I will put you in charge of many things. Come and share your master's happiness!

will achieve it; thinking will not get in the way. I can't see it but I believe it will happen. GO will take over and YOU will begin to accomplish your goals. The Bible says, Without Faith, it is impossible to please God. Being that God has a reputation of being extremely wise; shouldn't YOU believe in YOU also?

10. Do surround yourself with positive people and say positive things.

People around you should bring you up and support your dreams. I would go out on a limb and say the more positive people around you the more positive you will be. Some important things to remember when you are choosing those closest to you are: Are they there during the good and the bad? How bad do they talk about others because they will talk about you? Are they an attribute to others in their life? Also are you saying positive things about others and what can you say positive to encourage yourself. Since you are making goals that will impact your life you want to make sure they are protected by surrounding yourself with a positive support team.

Who are the positive people in your life?

_____

_____

11. Do recognize your habits

Do you have a tendency to always get tired around 10 PM every night? Are people continuously telling you that your home is always immaculate? Have you ever noticed anyone admiring your car while you were not looking? Sometimes the things you love to do or the things you hate to do can help you with your goals. For instance, if you hate being up at night, wouldn't that be the worst time to try to accomplish the goal of cleaning your room or doing your laundry? If your goal is to start your own business wouldn't it be important to notice what others appreciate you for or what you enjoy? Also this Do is important in relationships. I say this because if you make a certain goal to be successful in a relationship and in the past you have failed continuously, maybe you should take a second and note why. Recognize if there are any habits forming and go about correcting yourself if you have any bad, avoidable habits.

What are your good habits?

_____

_____

What are your bad habits?

_____

_____

12. Do be a good example

The reason this is such an excellent goal is because to be a good example you have to be applying these standards of goals. What is the point of having all the knowledge and not actually putting it to use? Being a good example allows you to help others by being a goal getter. You accomplish your goals and others praise you for your progress.

Who looks up to you?

_____

a. What attributes do you want them to see in you?

_____

b. What attributes do you need to work on and what exercises can you do?

_____

_____

Who do you look up to?

_____

_____

_____

13. *"PK" Moment: Do abstain from sex.*

Ladies and Gentlemen, This is exactly what you need to hear if you are single, young or old. If you have children or are in relationship and are single, do abstain. I have lived a sexual life that I am not particularly proud of. I wanted to wait until I was married to have sex, however, I gave into temptation.

I have a daughter, and I had a lot of healing to do emotionally because of the soul ties I made. I also ended up being single, emotionally struggling, and a new mother. There was a piece of me that didn't want to get married because they may not meet up to past relationships. It used to be an addiction for me. I was so happy before "doing it" but felt guilty afterward. I am now practicing abstaining and it has changed my life. If I meet someone who I like but then they show me a side of them that I do not need in my life, I have the power to let them go. We are no longer tied in the spirit. I also realize I am free spiritually to love God with all my heart. I only answer to God. I am not one with anyone but God. I have prospered spiritually. I am the youth pastor at my church. This is a goal I always wanted and by living focused, free, and holy I am able to hold such an office. Last but not least, the first man I actually said lets have a real relationship; no sex became the first man who truly loved me and desired to please me. The first guy who wants to marry me, not just talk but action. Do you think it has anything do with the "abstaining from sex commandment?"

14. Do organize yourself

I went out and bought the idiot's guide to organizing your life. I take this very seriously because in business and goal setting it is important to have things in order. In everything in life there is order set up and I believe strongly to be a successful goal achiever you must have order in your life. Think about it…

"PK" Moment: Even God almighty says we need to be in order and decently Romans 13:13.

If you show up to a meeting with a potential client and everything is out of order and you have no presentation, how will this affect your goal?

If you bring a potential mate to your home and there are dishes in your sink, clothes on your floor, you haven't dusted in a year. How do you think your goal to get married will size up? Trust me no man or woman wants to clean up after you.

Are you organized?

_____

_____

How can you improve your room? Office?

_____

_____

Do you have a filing cabinet?

_____

_____

15. Do improve every day

Improve means to get a little better, take a step higher, or just do more. It is important that you have evidence that things are getting better. You can see it in your decisions, actions, character, and goals crossed off. For instance, my goal is to be a full-time professional speaker and author. Each day I write more in my book so the book is being perfected. I am constantly attending Toastmasters weekly to sharpen my speaking ability. I am improving everyday and I would encourage everyone to take a stride daily. I noticed that reading books and praying is impacting internally so much that my external decisions are improving.

What else can you do to achieve your goals?

_____

_____

What organizations would help you improve yourself?

_____

_____

a.) Do they cost?

_____

_____

b.) Are you willing to pay that amount?

_____

_____

10   *Practical Places*

1. Car

2. Refrigerator

3. Desk

4. Look into creative computer programs

5. E-mail yourself or have a reminder sent to you

6. Put your goals on a screen saver

7. Audibly record your goals. Most cell phones have voice record

8. Write it on paper and tape it to your computer

9. T-Shirt

10. Picture frame

What are some other ideas of places you could place you goals?

_____

_____

Where is the craziest place you could ever place your goal?

_____

_____

20 Powerful Parallels

Every shot counts, every second matters, every opportunity is priceless. What do you do when the odds are stacked against you? How bad do you want to win? What do you do when you are the underdog? At times it takes more effort to win than other times. How do you keep trying when you are being defeated? The game of basketball is intense and it has a lot of great principles. I will touch twenty.

1. Follow through (Perseverance)

You will not make consistent shots without a proper follow through. The reason you are told to follow through when shooting a basketball is so the next time you can correct what you did wrong. If done correctly you will achieve a high level of accuracy.

Think about the sport of basketball. It is the goal made that gets you excited. When you follow through properly with goals you will have consistent achievement. On the court, if you follow through you will start making more shots because you know where the shot is going. It takes practice and eventually comes natural. Follow through is paralleled with goals because of achievement and consequence. It is exciting to make your goals one after another.

2. Nutrition (Consistency and daily routine)

By being nutritious and watching your daily intake your game will excel. Daily consistency makes it easier for the slam-dunk. In basketball you have to eat correctly and make sure you are not overweight. You have to watch your sugar and watch your caloric intake. With goals you also need to watch your daily intake.

What is going into your spirit and heart daily?

_____

_____

Is it encouragement or discouragement?

_____

_____

Who are you hanging around?

_____

_____

Do you and that person have similar goals and dreams?

_____

_____

Are your goals written down?

_____

_____

Do you consume them daily?

_____

_____

What is your daily intake?

_____

_____

3. Form is everything (Presence and Integrity)
What do you tell others on the court if your shot is ugly? There is a slam-dunk contest every year that is judging slam-dunks in basketball. Remember style point's count. It is not just how you do it but the way you do it. In goals you have to remember that you are being watched and analyzed. Now that you are reaching new heights style points count. You can not just go after your goals anymore but you have to do it right and with style.

4. Starter vs. Second String (Prioritizing)
When getting picked for any basketball team it is everyone's goal to be a starter. This symbolizes that you are in the top 5 and your coach has confidence that you will get the game off to a great start. Second string members are found on the bench. These are the members of the team who play second. Both are good and necessary for the team but the starters are the best and most seasoned.

With goals you can look at it two ways. First, some of your goals are going to take priority over others. Some are going to take the bench sometimes. Second, you have to be a starter. It's easier to just sit on the bench and not have too much responsibility, but a starter has to take initiative and responsibility. That is what you have to do when it comes to goals. Be a starter, take it serious, and play hard.

5. Warm-Up (Endurance, Patience, and Staying Power)
The warm-up is pre-game and it is built to help endure the game. To get warmed up is to prepare you.
Endurance works two ways:

1. You have to endure what people say. Everyone is not going to be on your side and agree with your goals however, you must endure the negativity to get to the manifestation of your goals. You have to stand up for yourself. Others may not know the drive you have or the dreams put in your heart. You must endure. Be confident in your goal.

2. You can't afford to get tired in the last quarter. When the game is going good and the defense of the other team is tight, points are scarce. You may be the last one available to shoot the 3-pointer. You can't be tired. The alley-oop may be right there but if you haven't endured. How are you going to slam dunk? Just like goals, if you are right there. You have worked hard and kept the faith. The goal may be one step away but because you didn't endure, you missed out.

6. Pow-Wow Chant (Encouragement)
Most Pow-Wow's are in the middle of the floor pre- and post- game. Everyone is getting pumped up before the big game and totally excited. With goals you cannot lose the excitement. Your passion is your drive. So you can have a personal pow-wow or gather a team of people to get you re-energized.

7. Defense (Defending Yourself)
You have to guard your goal so the other team cannot score. Same in life, guard your goals. You don't want someone to score on you and you sure do not want someone to take away your dream and dribble away. Protect your goals by not telling everyone just like you want to protect the ball. And there is always the trash-talker who comes up in the midst of the game and says how bad you are going to do. Defend yourself and your dream however, remember you have the goods and don't waste your time.

8. Missed shots (Mistakes)

Missed shots are where the learning comes in so do not be discouraged. You learn what you are doing wrong. You learn how to use the backboard if needed. When it comes to having a goal, you may have every intention to make it but fall short.

First attempt you may miss the shot or goal but even if you miss it, you need to try again. Sometimes you may miss it twice, three, or four times but you must learn from your mistakes and strive to correct whatever you did wrong. Do your follow-through and warm up. Also watch your daily intake. If you are ever down, call for a pow-wow. Missed shots hurt.

9. Bench-Warmer (Encouraging others and Being Humble)

I've sat the bench. My dad taught me how to play b-ball in the 6th grade and there were a lot of girls who were better than me but I still loved the game. I ended up sitting the bench a lot and as I reflect back I remember doing the cheers with the cheerleaders. Every time the players who were in the game took a seat we had to stand up and cheer.

One thing about being a bench warmer is you learn how to cheer for others. You also learn a lot about the game. While making your goals you can get to know people who have already attained them and watch how they did it. Remember cheer for others and they will cheer for you to accomplish your goals. Your time is coming.

Side Note: You better be ready when you get off the bench if you want to stay in the game. It applies to goals because once you begin to be successful, help and cheer for others, be ready at all times.

10. Half-time (Evaluation)

Half-time comes and your team is either winning or losing however half-time is designated to help you evaluate your course so far. It is a quick time to reflect on the game. What are you doing well? What are you doing badly? With your goals sometimes it is good to re-evaluate whether or not you are making effective goals. Are you achieving your goals or are you just staring at them. It could be every year on your birthday or every pay day. It could be every Sunday morning or the 30th of each month. You have to evaluate your goals and progress but it is totally your choice, when.

When is your time for evaluation?

_____

_____

What are you going to evaluate?

_____

_____

11. Over-time (Composure)

Over-time is good because most likely you played a good, hard game. However, if you make it to over-time your good was not good enough and the game is tied. Over-time is extra time to gain points and win. In this time you have to put everything on the line. You have to give your all in all. Just like goals, you have to give it your all and keep your composure even after you have been stretched.

12. Game Book (Preparation)

Every player on a team has to have a game book. You keep a game book to know how to activate the plays. With goals you can create a game book consisting of your goals or just list your goals. This game book called "You Goal Girl" will show you how to complete your goals. With a game book usually your coach, someone with a lot more experience will teach and develop these plays. When you are developing goals sometimes it is tremendously more helpful if you receive feedback from someone more experienced. To prepare to be a top achiever it is important to develop a game book.

13. Tip-off (Time)

The tip-off is used to get the game started. Two of the most athletic on the team line up to tip the ball to one of their members to see who gets to begin the game with the ball. You are probably wondering what this has to do with goals but it is awesome. The tip-off is at the beginning, so if you miss it you still have the whole game to recover. The beginning isn't everything; it is how you can finish. The tip-off can help you get a good start but do not be discouraged if missed, you have a long way and a lot of opportunities to go.

14. Foul Out (Re-focus)

It can be depressing. It can really make you want to give up. A foul out is when you have 5 fouls. In basketball you are only permitted 4 fouls and 5 exceeds.

When you fouled out in basketball, you have made silly mistakes or made an inappropriate move and because of this you have to sit on the bench the rest of the game whether 1 quarter or 3 quarters…at least, until the next game. This is where goals come in. Just like fouling out sometimes we exceed the amount of mistakes we are allotted for one goal. We then have to make another goal or in basketball terms await the next game.

I wanted to be student government president but instead I didn't focus on that one goal but was involved in 6 other clubs. My focus was in other places. Therefore, I still became president, just not of the student government. These are the choices you have to make for yourself. However, remember to be serious about your goals and try to stay focused.

15. Free Throws (Focus and Routine)

Free Throws are given to you after you have been fouled. It is a free shot. Sometimes the difference between making and missing this shot is simply focus. People are depending on you to increase the advantage with increased points. With goals you must stay focused.

On the other hand, to prepare to be a great free throw shooter you must have a routine to be successful. Sometimes the player walks up to the line, bounces the ball three times, and dips then follow-through to make the shot. Someone else may just bounce once and shoot. Whatever your routine, it is valuable to have a consistent pattern and practice daily.

16. Crowd (Following and Fans)

So many athletes and famous people say what drives them is their fans. Their motivation is the crowd cheering for them when they walk on the court. The cheers from the crowd motivate them. With goals it is good to always identify what motivates you and excites you. Does it motivate you when people give you accolades? Is that why you want success so bad?

Also, realize that there are people following and cheering for you and if you consider that sometimes decision-making is easier. Identify your crowd and thank them.

Who are your fans?

_____

_____

17.   Hustle (Dedication)

According to thesaurus.com, hustle means to apply oneself, push, race, concentrate, dedicate, be diligent, buckle down, and energy. Just like the game of basketball you have to hustle. The coach is the one who usually screams this. When I was on the court and I was getting tired after the first 5-10 minutes playing. I started to feel my lungs expanding and the speed I had before was slowly diminishing. It was then when I heard a loud "HUSTLE!" With your goals you have to "HUSTLE" with energy and diligence it is important to achieve your goals. Even when you get tired or fatigue, you must HUSTLE.

18. Crossover and Crossover (Creativity)

When a basketball game is on TV there is always a crossover. You might notice a short, quick move that left the opponent behind. The crowd usually begins to get hyped up and this is exactly what happens in goal-setting. There is a crowd cheering for you, hyping you to succeed. Sometimes to get them back involved or to get the momentum you have to crossover.

19. Man-to-Man vs. Zone (Attitude)

Man-to-Man is a type of defense that is so serious. When it is time to "man up" there are no excuses allowed. You are responsible for your man and if you can't keep up, you are responsible. With man to man you cannot worry about those around you. Another type of Defense is Zone and this is a more laid back approach. It is more of a team-oriented defense where everyone is watching each others back.

I would encourage you to "man up." With goals the hands on approach is the answer because you have to take responsibility. No one can take care of your goals like you can.

20. Slam Dunk (Reward)

When you can dunk you have attained the points, the crowd, the physical ability, and the evidence of daily practice. Slam Dunk is your reward for working hard. The Slam Dunk is your opportunity to do something special. You get a chance to enjoy the moment. It is your moment. No one can take your joy and later no one can take the credit unless someone assisted you and of course they should get credit for helping you attain. SLAM DUNK YOUR GOALS! (Remember style point's count)

Every shot counts, every second matters, every opportunity is priceless. What do you do when the odds are stacked against you? How bad do you want to win? What do you do when you are the underdog? (At times it takes more effort to win than other times) How do you keep trying when you are being defeated?

_____

_____

10 *Go Affirmations*

1. I will celebrate my progress but still make a commitment to progress.

2. I will continue to go for my goals even after that deadline is missed; I can't be stopped.

3. Today I will complete a goal; I will not procrastinate any more.

4. You Goal Girl!

5. I will ignore all pessimism and encourage myself if needed.

6. Check out my goals, they are everywhere. You cannot take them away because they are inside of me and they will become manifested.

7. I will cover great goals in all areas of my life and continue to excel.

8. I will go today, not tomorrow, because today is the day to make it happen. I have to take the first step!

9. I will not give up and I will continue to achieve my goals.

10. I will praise the Lord.

Add your own affirmations

_____

_____

_____

_____

_____

_____

_____

You Goal Girl!
Begin Here:

The following pages are to be used as a Sketch Pad to a Wise Artist. The Artist would 1st Quick-Draw an Idea or Desire on the Sketch Pad. After Careful Analyzing —you would *then* begin Painting on the Fine Canvas.

•   •   •

Wise Artist ~ Can Be You
Sketch Book ~ The To-Do List / Goals In Writing
Fine Canvas ~ Life —Your Life

By: Elijah Blue
The Expressionaire

Today's Goals:

Short Term Goals:
within 6 months

_____

_____

_____

_____

_____

_____

_____

_____

_____

_____

_____

_____

_____

_____

_____

_____

_____

_____

_____

_____

_____

_____

Long Term Goals:

_____
_____
_____
_____
_____
_____
_____
_____
_____
_____
_____
_____
_____
_____
_____
_____
_____
_____
_____
_____
_____
_____
_____
_____
_____